it is my prayer
that something in
this book motivates
you to desire a greater
relationship with the Lord

Sister Benetta Perry
2021

# FROM HIS WORD TO MY HEART

*Discovering the Will of God*

BENETTA PERRY

Disclaimer: This is a work of fiction. Names, characters, businesses, places, events, locales, and incidents are either the products of the author's imagination or used in a fictitious manner. Any resemblance to actual persons, living or dead, or actual events is purely coincidental.

Scripture quotations marked as (AMP) are taken from the Amplified Bible Copyright © 1954, 1958, 1962, 1964, 1965, 1987, 1999-2015 by The Lockman Foundation

Scripture quotations marked as (KJV) are taken from the King James Version of the Bible by Public Domain

Scripture quotations marked as (MSG) are taken from THE MESSAGE Copyright © by Eugene H. Peterson 1993, 1994, 1995, 1996, 2000, 2001, 2002, 2018. Used by permission of NavPress Publishing Group. All rights reserved. Represented by Tyndale House Publishers, Inc.

Scripture quotations marked as (NLT) are taken from The Holy Bible, New Living Translation, Copyright © 1996, 2004, 2007, 2015 by Tyndale House Foundation. Used by permission of Tyndale House Publishers, Inc., Carol Stream, Illiniois 60188. All rights reserved.

Scripture quotations marked as (NLV) are taken from New Living Version Copyright © 1969 and 2003. Used by permission of Barbour Publishing, Inc., Uhrichsville, Ohio 44683. All rights reserved.

Printed in the United States of America

First Printing, 2019

Print ISBN: 978-1-54398-457-6
eBook ISBN: 978-1-54398-458-3

Published by Bookbaby
7905 N. Crescent Blvd
Pennsauken, NJ 08110

www.bookbaby.com

*This book is dedicated to my Lord and
Savior Jesus Christ, who I am grateful and
thankful to, for the vision He gave to me.*

*To my Sister, Teresa, my Sons, Joey Jr and
Jonathan, my Daughter, Rochelle. I thank you
all for believing in God's anointing upon my life,
verbally encouraging me to walk in the spiritual gift
given to me and for constantly praying for me.*

*To my Mother and Father, Pastor Benjamin D. &
Isabell U. Blake – without you there would be no me.*

*It is my prayer that this personal study guide
will bless, stretch and deliver all who read it.*

# TABLE OF CONTENTS

# Discovering the Will of God

## The Mission

The purpose of this book is to help you get a better understanding of how to live your life in the will of God. For years, I've heard it said that most Christians do not do the will of God because they do not know the will of God. Prayerfully, this book will help to turn this saying around, for you, as it did for me.

## The Journey

As you progress thru this book, you will notice that although the theme of this book is about the will of God, hopefully, it will be revealed to you that this book is really about you dying to yourself. When you love someone, you want to please them and in pleasing them, it brings you pleasure. Since we love God, we want to please Him and in order to please Him, we must do His will, and in doing His will, it will in turn bring us joy.

# PREFACE

As a child, I loved to read. Since my childhood, until now, I have read through the Bible many times. However, during most of my early years, when I read the Bible, it felt as if I were reading any other interesting book. During my quick ritualistic routine of morning readings, time stood still, as it seemed to take forever to get through a few verses, much less an entire chapter. Nearly a decade had passed before I was able to read a full chapter during a morning session. As I got older, I was taught that I needed to spend quality time with God in order to develop a deeper relationship with Him. It was then my desire to spend more time with the Lord grew. However, I began to get frustrated because it seemed that my morning readings would never make it to five minutes of time with the Lord. I did not realize that, before now, I was only reading the Bible, I was not having quality time with the Lord. I desperately wanted to develop my own personal devotional time with the Lord, but I did not know how. I was clueless but determined. As a result, I started asking around. I polled other Christians as to what their morning devotion looked like. How did they spend quality time with the Lord? How long did their quality time with the Lord last? What a disastrous plan that was! I got a huge range of answers. All of my polling efforts only proved to further confuse me. I eventually came to realize that I could not mimic another person's relationship with the Lord. I needed to seek His face for myself. Thus, my prayer for myself was "Lord teach me how to commune with you".

My desire was to have a better understanding of God's word. I wanted to hear from the Lord. I needed to hear from the Lord. My desire was to have more of Jesus' traits and less of my traits. Once I asked the Holy Spirit to teach me how to have quiet quality time with the Lord, things eventually started to change. The more I prayed and read, I noticed that the Holy Spirit was opening up my understanding. This was a process. A slow process, but a steadily improving process. I began to be encouraged. I also began to study God's Word corporately through attending Sunday School and Bible Study. I was afforded many opportunities to teach and through my study and teachings, more of God's word was revealed to me. As a result, my morning readings were being transformed into morning devotions. I was truly experiencing quality time with the Lord. As I read God's Word, my eyes would light up with each page. Time passed quickly. Each morning, as I immersed myself into God's Word, I was lost in time. Sometimes, I got so caught up, I just had to make myself stop reading. When I read the Bible, I got excited and my need to share what I read began to bubble up within me. It was like fire shut up in my bones. I could not wait to share the revelation with someone, anyone, everyone. For me, this experience showed me the difference between reading and revelation.

How did this personal Bible devotional series come about? Glad you asked. God speaks thru His word. So, from His mouth to my heart, the more I read and meditated upon the Lord's word, the more I began to absorb His word into my heart and less into my head. I began to develop a stronger heart relationship, with the Lord, in addition to my existing head relationship. I heard in my spirit, from God's word to my heart. Thus, the title of this series "From His Word to My Heart".

# INTRODUCTION

For years, as a babe in Christ, I struggled with finding the will of God for my life. Today, I talk to many Christians who also struggle with finding the will of God for their lives. We hear it said all the time, "I do not know what the will of God is for me". I believe, what is really meant, is "I do not know what God's purpose and plan is for my life". Thru the scriptures, we will learn that the will of God is made clear in His word. His will applies to each and every one of His children, equally. If we concentrate more on actively living according to His will in our lives, then, in God's timing, the rest will come. We should all try not to focus on the cloudy or grey areas in God's word but instead walk boldly and consistently according to the clear blue skies of His word. Living and thinking in this manner, will eliminate much frustration and confusion that exist between Christians.

Why do the will of God? Because deep down we, as Christians, desire to be obedient to His Word. Why do we want to be obedient to His Word, because ultimately, we want the blessings of God to be poured out abundantly into our lives and into the lives of our loved ones.

We are given a priceless gift in exchange for our obedience. We are given a gift that cannot be bought with money. What is this gift? Glad you asked. The gift is the Holy Ghost, given to those who obey.

> Acts 5:32 (KJV) "And we are his witnesses of these things; and so is also the Holy Ghost, whom God hath given to them that obey him".

> Acts 5:32 (NLT) "We are witnesses of these things and so is the Holy Spirit, who is given by God to those who obey him".

> Acts 5:32 (MSG) "And we are witnesses to these things. The Holy Spirit, whom God gives to those who obey him, corroborates every detail".

In this book, I will share with you some nuggets of revelations that spoke to me and prayerfully, they will speak to you as well. Let's begin our morning breakfast nuggets. I hope that you have your coffee, milk, tea, water, or juice in hand. I do.

> Psalms 34:8(KJV) "O taste and see that the Lord is good; blessed is the man that trusteth in him"

> Psalms 34:8(NLT) "Taste and see that the Lord is good. Oh, the joys of those who take refuge in him!"

> Psalms 34:8(MSG) "Open your mouth and taste, open your eyes and see how good God is. Blessed are you who run to him."

# Nugget 01: Flee Fornication

What is the will of God for my life? Let us explore some scriptures that state the will of God for our lives.

> 1 Thessalonians 4:3 (KJV) "For this is the will of God, even your sanctification, that ye should abstain from fornication".

> 1 Thessalonians 4:3 (NLT) "God's will is for you to be holy, so stay away from all sexual sin".

> 1 Thessalonians 4:3 (MSG) "God wants you to live a pure life. Keep yourselves from sexual promiscuity".

Here is the will of God, simply put, no sex outside of marriage. Period.

**Examples - Legal disclaimer: Situations described, and names used are fictitious. Any similarity to your life is purely coincidental and divine.**

> Sister Cali's husband of 15 years died. Sister Cali started attending the Grief Counseling meetings, held on Wednesday nights, at church. During one of the sessions, she caught the eye of Brother Willi, whose wife of 30 years died of cancer. After

the meetings, they would hang out and talk in the church parking lot. Eventually, their friendship progressed to meeting at a coffee shop after the grief counseling sessions ended. They are both senior citizens, about 65 or more years old+, collecting their retirement benefits plus their spouse's social security benefits. Now, a few years down the road, they have found love again and are in a committed relationship. Neither thought they would experience happiness again. They thank God each day for blessing them with each other. They are thankful to the Grief Counseling ministry for helping them to see life after the death of their spouses. On the other hand, they are now faced with a life altering dilemma. If they marry, their financial benefits would be cut drastically. It is taught over and over that financial struggles are the #1 reason for divorce. It seems that their chance at sustained happiness is greater, if they remain single. From time to time, they are intimate, but not too often however.

Teri Rene graduated top in her high school class. She was the 1st place winner of her church college scholarship contest. The grand prize was their financial support for 4 years, as long as she maintained at least a B average. Making and maintaining a B average was no problem for Teri, as she proudly made the dean's list, each semester. She was very active in the College Students for Christ Organization.

She met the president of the organization, Matt. After a few months of dating, they became a couple. They both agreed that they do not want anything to interfere with the continuing of their education. They are very responsible and always keep safe sex as their primary focus. They always use a condom. They are young and in love. Everyone their age is doing it, and it is really no big deal.

Cherise is a divorcee. Her husband cheated on her. They had a horrible sex life. She wants to have a great relationship with her new husband inside and outside of the bedroom. The Lord has finally bought her Boaz. Her Boaz proposed marriage to her and she accepted. They are now formally engaged, with a wedding date set for the next year. They are going to marriage counselling. However, being sexually compatible is very important to her for having a lasting and fulfilling marriage. They are intimate only to try things out. They plan to stop and save themselves for the wedding night, but they just wanted to make sure. Getting married will make everything right.

Lori and Paul are childhood sweethearts. Neither are saved. They moved in together after high school. They have two children. They both have good jobs and are very loyal and happy. One day, some of the local church members came to witness to them and invite them to church. They accepted the offer and attended the services. Eventually, both gave their lives to Christ. However, they see no need to get a piece of paper. Getting a marriage license would change nothing in their lives or their relationship. They have been and will continue to be very committed to one another. They have been shacking for over 15 years. Their state recognizes common law marriage, as a result, they are legally married. They see no problem.

Perhaps one of these examples walked down your street or the street of a friend or family member. There is no need to debate nor give further clarification on this point because we all know what sex means. In this discussion of sex, I have intentionally not mentioned self-gratification nor oral sex. Why? Because those discussion points are brought up by some only to try to find a loophole to get to the end result without getting there by God's means and methods. Abstaining from fornication is not cloudy nor grey but a clear blue-sky directive – will of God. For many, just obeying this command, might take a lifetime. As a single, Christian, abstinence is the will of God.

## Prayer of Repentance

Lord, I thank You for my life. I thank You for my loved ones. I thank You for Jesus standing in the gap for my sins. Forgive me for fornication. Give me a distaste for that which does not bring You honor. Holy Spirit give me the self-control and strength that I need to fight my fleshly desires both mentally and physically. Lord, change me, my mind and my heart so that I only want to engage in Godly, God honoring sex! Lord give me the desire to be with the one I love in intimacy as You created it to be. Lord, I thank You for Your patience and Your love towards me. Holy Spirit, I stand on the toes of anticipation of living a new life, one that is pleasing to my Lord. This prayer I pray, in the name of Jesus Christ. Amen.

# NUGGET 02: RENEW YOUR MIND

What is the will of God for my life? Let us explore some scriptures that state the will of God for our lives.

Romans 12:1-2 (KJV) "I beseech you therefore, brethren, by the mercies of God, that ye present your bodies a living sacrifice, holy, acceptable unto God, which is your reasonable service. And be not conformed to this world: but be ye transformed by the renewing of your mind, that ye may prove what is that good, and acceptable, and perfect, will of God."

Romans 12:1-2 (NLT) "And so, dear brothers and sisters, I plead with you to give your bodies to God because of all he has done for you. Let them be a living and holy sacrifice, the kind he will find acceptable. This is truly the way to worship him. Don't copy the behavior and customs of this world, but let God transform you into a new person by changing the way you think. Then you will learn to know God's will for you, which is good and pleasing and perfect."

Romans 12:1-2 (MSG) "So here's what I want you to do, God helping you: Take your everyday, ordinary life, your sleeping, eating, going to work, and walking around life, and place it before God as an offering. Embracing what God does for you is the best thing you can do for him. Don't become so well adjusted to your culture that you fit into it without even thinking. Instead, fix your attention on God. You'll be changed from the inside out. Readily recognize what he wants from you, and quickly respond to it. Unlike the culture around you, always dragging you down to its level of immaturity, God brings the best out of you, develops well-formed maturity in you."

Here is the will of God for your life, simply put, renew your mind. What is the definition of renew? It means to begin again, to restore, to restore to a former state, to revive, to reestablish, to recover, to do again, and to replenish.

How can you live a victorious life, if you feed yourself poison every day? You can not. You will die from the inside out. Poison is a form of stinking thinking. In order to live a victorious life, you must have a renewing of your mind.

In order to renew your mind, you must apply the Word of God to your stinking thinking. Any lies fed to you from your own thoughts, family members, friends, or this sinful world, needs to be filtered through the Word of God. The Word of God tells us what to think.

> Philippians 4:8 (KJV) "Finally, brethren, whatsoever things are true, whatsoever things are honest, whatsoever things are just, whatsoever things are pure, whatsoever things are lovely, whatsoever things are of good report; if there be any virtue, and if there be any praise, think on these things."

> Philippians 4:8 (NLT) "And now, dear brothers and sisters, one final thing. Fix your thoughts on what is true, and honorable, and right, and pure, and lovely, and admirable. Think about things that are excellent and worthy of praise."

> Philippians 4:8 (MSG) "Summing it all up, friends, I'd say you'll do best by filling your minds and meditating on things true, noble, reputable, authentic, compelling, gracious – the best, not the worst; the beautiful, not the ugly; things to praise, not things to curse."

Your mind's stinking thinking – "I am ugly! I am worthless! I am nothing!"

Your renewed thought – "I am marvelous in God's eyes. It does not matter what others say."

> Psalms 139:14 (KJV) "I will praise thee, for I am fearfully and wonderfully made: marvelous are they works; and that my soul knoweth right well."

Psalms 139:14 (NLT) "Thank you for making me so wonderfully complex! Your workmanship is marvelous – how well I know it."

Psalms 139:14 (MSG) " I thank you, High God – you're breathtaking! Body and soul, I am marvelously made!"

Your mind's stinking thinking – "God does not care about me! God hates me!"

Your renewed thought – "God has a prosperous future for me – despite what my situation looks like today."

Jeremiah 19:11 (KJV) "For I know the thoughts that I think toward you, saith the Lord, thoughts of peace, and not of evil, to give you an expected end."

Jeremiah 29:11 (NLT) "For I know the plans I have for you, says the Lord. They are plans for good and not for disaster, to give you a future and a hope."

Jeremiah 29:11 (MSG) "I know what I'm doing. I have it all planned out – plans to take care of you, not abandon you, plans to give you the future you hope for."

I Peter 5:7 (KJV) "Casting all your care upon him: for he careth for you."

1 Peter 5:7 (NLT) "Give all your worries and cares to God, for he cares about you."

1 Peter 5:7 (AMP) "casting all your cares [all your anxieties, all your worries, and all your concerns, once and for all] on Him, for He cares about you [with deepest affection, and watches over you very carefully]"

Train your natural mind to know what your spirit man already knows - that is, the truth in God's Word. Once you change your thinking, then you can change your speaking. Know that even though you can't, God can. You have to learn to trust God more than you trust your own mind.

**Prayer of Help**

Heavenly Father, I thank You for creating me. Lord, I thank You for touching me with life each and every day. Lord, I thank You for your protection over my life. Holy Spirit touch my eyes and help me to see myself as You see me. Holy Spirit block the arrows of lies aimed at my self-esteem. When I look in the mirror, Lord let me see Your marvelous creation. This prayer, I pray in the name of Jesus Christ. Amen.

**Life Application: "What can I do to cultivate a renewed mind?"**

## Action Steps:

1. Each morning, look in the mirror and compliment yourself
2. Each night, before bed, look in the mirror and compliment yourself
3. Write down each compliment and each day do not repeat a compliment
4. At the end of the week, pray and thank God for loving you and creating such an amazing person – thanking God for each compliment that you wrote down

# NUGGET 03: INTEGRITY ON THE JOB

What is the will of God for my life? Let us explore some scriptures that state the will of God for our lives.

Ephesians 6:5-7(KJV) "Servants, be obedient to them that are your masters according to the flesh, with fear and trembling, in singleness of your heart, as unto Christ; Not with eye service, as men pleasers; but as the servants of Christ, doing the will of God from the heart; With good will doing service, as to the Lord, and not to men:"

Ephesians 6:5-7 (NLT) "Slaves, obey your earthly masters with deep respect and fear. Serve them sincerely as you would serve Christ. Try to please them all the time, not just when they are watching you. As slaves of Christ, do the will of God with all your heart. Work with enthusiasm, as though you were working for the Lord rather than for people."

Ephesians 6:5-7 (MSG) "Servants, respectfully obey your earthly masters but always with an eye to obeying the real master, Christ. Don't just do what you have to do to get by, but work heartily, as Christ's servants doing what God wants you to do. And work with a smile on your face, always keeping in mind that no matter who happens to be giving the orders, you're really serving God."

Here is the will of God for your life, simply put, obey all of the rules of your job. Obey the company rules. Some companies are very well organized and will provide a new employee with the company's rules during orientation. Some managers will tell their employees the rules of their specific job. Still yet, other managers will assume you know the common-sense rules and only tell you after the fact, that is, once you are about to get written up or possibly fired. In either situation, "I did not know", will not be a defense. You, the employee, are responsible to know the company's rules. This knowledge protects you. You can ask the human resource (HR) manager for an employee handbook or you can schedule a 1 on 1 meeting with your manager/supervisor and discuss the company's rules. There is never a reason for you not knowing the rules of the company you are employed by.

**Examples - Legal disclaimer: Situations described, and names used are fictitious. Any similarity to your life is purely coincidental and divine.**

Delilah has been on her job for 15 years. She knows the ins and outs of things and is very well respected.

Being one of the few senior employees, she believes that this type of loyalty surely comes with some personal perks. After she dedicated her life to Christ, she got involved more in church ministry and other church activities. This year, she is excited to be on the program committee for her church's Annual Women's Day. She needs to make 200 colored copies of the Women's Day program. Over the weekend, she went to her job, used their printer, and made the needed copies. She has put in the years and feels this is a great benefit. Plus, no one saw her. There are no cameras in the printer room. All is good. She has the copies and as an added benefit, will not have to use the funds from the program committee. Those funds can now be carried over and will increase next year's budget. This is the first time she has ever used the company's printer for personal copies. Other co-workers use the company printer to make personal copies all the time. One time in 15 years is really no big deal.

Breann has been on her job for two weeks. She was hired as the receptionist at a Dentist office. The office opens at 9 am. She is required to be at work at 8 am. She has always considered herself a night owl and a late morning sleeper. She cannot make it to work on time. However, she is always there by 8:30 am and she does not understand why her supervisor is threatening to write her up. Customers arrive at 9 am, and she is always there by 8:30 am. She does not see the problem and feels her supervisor is picking at her and just does not like her. The company's rule is, after 3 write ups, you can be fired. She really needs this job. Many of the customers give her compliments and most of the staff really like her. She has the perfect personality for this receptionist job. And to top it off, she loves her job. The office does not open for business until 9 am. She is always at her desk and ready, long before 9 am. There are no customers there waiting or see her arriving late. The staff arrives at 8 am, drink coffee and chit chat until 9 am. So, what is the big deal?

Chris is a single father of 4. He is doing the best he can working as a janitor. He looks for ways to make his money stretch, however, it is challenging given that he makes minimum wages. All of his children need school supplies. He cannot afford to buy each child what they need during the entire school year. Various organizations give school supplies, to the underprivileged and underserved children, however, this is only at the beginning of the school year. More is needed during the school year. The company he contracts with has a supply cabinet. Since he is one of the janitors, he has access to it. He observes employees coming in and out of the supply room, taking supplies from the cabinet, each and every day. Chris decided, when needed, to take home erasers, pencils, paper, glue, and tablets. He only takes what is needed, when it is needed and no extras. He is not being greedy nor wasteful. Whether the supplies are taken by the employees or Chris, it should not matter, the supplies are reduced, and no harm is done. The secretary takes inventory and reorders supplies each month.

If your action can not be done in the presence of your boss, then you know that action is wrong. God will not be pleased with any action you have to sneak to perform. If your action can not be visible to all, then your action is wrong.

Deep down, in our gut, we know right actions from wrong actions on our job. Sneaking with a co-worker will only last until that co-worker gets mad at you. Make our Lord happy by obeying your company's rules.

> Philippians 2:12-15 (KJV) "Wherefore, my beloved, as ye have always obeyed, not as in my presence only, but now much more in my absence, work out your own salvation with fear and trembling. For it is God which worketh in you both to will and to do of his good pleasure. Do all things without murmurings and disputings: That ye may be blameless and harmless, the sons of God, without rebuke, in the midst of a crooked and perverse nation, among whom ye shine as lights in the world."

Philippians 2:12-15 (NLT) "Dear friends, you always followed my instructions when I was with you. And now that I am away, it is even more important. Work hard to show the results of your salvation, obeying God with deep reverence and fear. For God is working in you, giving you the desire and the power to do what pleases him. Do everything without complaining and arguing, so that no one can criticize you. Live clean, innocent lives as children of God, shining like bright lights in a world full of crooked and perverse people."

Philippians 2:12-15 (MSG) "What I'm getting at, friends, is that you should simply keep on doing what you've done from the beginning. When I was living among you, you lived in responsive obedience. Now that I'm separated from you, keep it up. Better yet, redouble your efforts. Be energetic in your life of salvation, reverent and sensitive before God. That energy is God's energy, an energy deep within you, God himself willing and working at what will give him the most pleasure. Do everything readily and cheerfully, no bickering, no second-guessing allowed! Go out into the world uncorrupted, a breath of fresh air in this squalid and polluted society. Providing people with a glimpse of good living and of the living God."

The message here is clear, , as we work for our employers, we are to work for them, out of their eyesight, with the same integrity and service that we would give them, if they were standing and looking at us. True integrity is shown at all times, whether you are alone or in a crowded room.

> Colossians 3:22-23 (KJV) "Servants, obey in all things your masters according to the flesh; not with eyeservice, as men pleasures; but in singleness of heart, fearing God: And whatsoever ye do, do it heartily, as to the Lord, and not unto men;"

> Colossians 3:22-23 (NLT) "Slaves, obey your earthly masters in everything you do. Try to please them all the time, not just when they are watching you. Serve them sincerely because of your reverent fear of the Lord. Work willingly at whatever you do, as though you were working for the Lord rather than for people."

> Colossians 3:22-23 (MSG) "Servants, do what you're told by your earthly masters. And don't just do the minimum that will get you by. Do your best."

God is our Provider. We are stewards. The job is our blessing. The Lord knows all and sees all. We can not hide from Him. Our Lord is looking, and He cares what you are doing. So, let's be mindful to work as if we were working for Him, because we are. Each day on your job, make a commitment to do the will of God.

Proverbs 5:21 (KJV) "For the ways of man are before the eyes of the Lord, and he pondereth all his goings."

Proverbs 5:21 (NLT) "For the Lord sees clearly what a man does, examining every path he takes."

Proverbs 5:21 (MSG) "Mark well that God doesn't miss a move you make, he's aware of every step you take."

## Prayer of Repentance

Heavenly Father, thank You for being, Jehovah Jireh, my Provider. Thank You for blessing me with this job. Thank You for Jesus standing in the gap for my sins. Heavenly Father forgive me for not honoring You in this position. Forgive me Lord for stealing time and stealing things, because stealing does not bring You honor. Lord give me a distaste for that which does not bring You honor. Holy Spirit give me the discipline to honor my employer as I would honor my Lord. This prayer, I pray in the name of Jesus Christ, Amen.

# Nugget 04: Thankful Heart

What is the will of God for my life? Let us explore some scriptures that state the will of God for our lives.

> I Thessalonians 5:17-19 (KJV) "Pray without ceasing. In everything give thanks: for this is the will of God in Christ Jesus concerning you. Quench not the Spirit."

> I Thessalonians 5:17-19 (NLT) "Never stop praying. Be thankful in all circumstances, for this is God's will for you who belong to Christ Jesus. Do not stifle the Holy Spirit."

> I Thessalonians 5:16-19 (MSG) "Be cheerful no matter what; pray all the time; thank God no matter what happens. This is the way God wants you who belong to Christ Jesus to live. Don't suppress the Spirit."

Here is the will of God for your life, simply put, give thanks "in" everything. Everything means everything. Everything does not mean somethings. Notice the scripture says give thanks "in" not give thanks "for". Come what may, in life, we need the power of God's Holy Spirit to comfort us and get us thru it, thus it is His will for us not to quench the Spirit.

**Examples - Legal disclaimer: Situations described, and names used are fictitious. Any similarity to your life is purely coincidental and divine.**

Sister Sharyn was born and raised in the church and has been on every committee there is. She was the President of the Street Ministry for 10 years. She is so faithful. During a doctor's visit, she was told that she had breast cancer. How can this be? Is this her reward for all her faithful service? What is there to be cheerful about? She desperately needs the comfort of the saints and God's Holy Spirit, now more than ever.

Paul Simon has been pastoring for 25 years at what is called a megachurch. Last week, he and first Lady Megan, lost their only child. Trudy, their precious 17-year-old daughter, just got her driver's license less than 6 months ago. Tragically, she was involved in a car wreck and died. How can this be? Is this his reward for all of his faithful service? What is there to be thankful about? They desperately need the comfort of their congregation and God's Holy Spirit, now more than ever.

Dean and Charla Lewis have been married for 5 years. They have been to many fertility specialist and Sister Charla has undergone surgery as well as tried all types of fertility treatments. They have spent $50,000 on trying to have a family, with no success. They are financially broke and broken hearted. How can this be? There is nothing to be thankful about. They desperately need the comfort of their family, friends, and God's Holy Spirit, now more than ever.

His will for us, to pray without ceasing, means we should each have a daily personal prayer life so that when a crisis happens, and sooner or later it will happen, we are reminded and thankful that we are not alone in that crisis.

We must believe and stand on God's Word – where He states – we will never be alone. The Holy Spirit is always with us, to comfort us.

John 14:16 (KJV) "And I will pray the Father, and he shall give you another Comforter, that he may abide with you forever."

John 14:16(NLT) "And I will ask the Father, and he will give you another Advocate, who will never leave you."

John 14:16(MSG) "If you love me, show it by doing what I've told you. I will talk to the Father, and he'll provide you another Friend so that you will always have someone with you. This Friend is the Spirit of Truth."

Hebrew 13:5(KJV) "Let your conversation be without covetousness; and be content with such things as ye have: for he hath said, I will never leave thee, nor forsake thee."

Hebrew 13:5(NLT) "Don't love money; be satisfied with what you have. For God has said, I will never fail you. I will never abandon you."

Hebrew 13:5(MSG) "Don't be obsessed with getting more material things. Be relaxed with what you have. Since God assured us, I'll never let you down, never walk off and leave you."

Let's look at each situation again and see if we can find a point of view to show thankfulness. Let's discover how they can "suffer well".

Sister Sharyn has been given a diagnosis and not necessarily a death sentence. She could ask her ministry members to fast and pray with her, prior to her starting chemotherapy. She should speak life to herself, educate herself and possibly become an advocate for early breast detection at her church. At her chemotherapy sessions, she could be the beacon of light to those around her. She could give them hope of deliverance from Cancer by being a witness of what the Lord can do. She could pray for everyone that steps into her room. Sister Sharyn can be thankful for this opportunity to minister to and pray for many hurting people. These are just a few ways how she can suffer well, even in the midst of her crisis.

Pastor Paul & Megan Simon are heart broken and will need to stand on God's word and fight against the spirit of anger, bitterness and depression. They should seek counseling from other Pastors. Once they are emotionally strong, they could fast and pray and ask the Lord's guidance in opening up their hearts to love again. They could explore adoption and become an advocate for adoption at their church. Pastor Paul & Megan can be thankful that they could give a lost child, intentional love. There is a child who needs a parent, and they are parents needing a child. A divine match. Thru their megachurch, many children could find Christian loving homes. This is truly something to be thankful for. They can turn their pain into purpose. This is just an avenue of how they can suffer well even in the aftermath of their crisis.

Dean and Charla are still both employed. That is a point of thankfulness. They could sit down and re-budget, cutting down and cutting back, in order to start saving again. They both work 8 am – 5pm and could each find part time evening work – agreeing to put all of that they earn from the part-time job into a Savings account. With prayer, the Lewis' could start a day care at their local church, or even start a day care as a business. The Lewis' could go on a year long foreign mission (like to Kenya) to help raise orphaned children. They could pour themselves into ministry and allow the Lord to move in their lives as He desires to do so. Taking the focus off of having their own baby could be helpful as they help care for other babies. It has been said when a couple suffers from infertility, after adoption, the wife then becomes pregnant. The key was in changing their focus and taking the stress off of their relationship. Sex could again be fun and enjoyable as opposed to a method mainly for reproduction. They can be thankful for an opportunity to partner in loving other babies. These are just a few ways in which they can suffer well in the midst of their crisis.

**Prayer of Hope Restored**

Heavenly Father forgive me for having my eyes on my situation and my hope in man. Lord, strengthen my heart and lift up my bowed down head. Holy Spirit restore the joy of life back within me. Lord, help me to give You praise in the storm. Forgive me as I took my eyes off of the prize of the cross and allowed the rocky road on this life's journey to sidetrack my hope and enthusiasm for life and kingdom building.

**Life Application: "What can I do to cultivate a thankful heart?"**

**Action Steps:**

1. For 1 week, each day, write down 1 thing or person that you are thankful for in your life?
2. At the end of the week, pray a prayer of thankfulness to God for each of the things or people you wrote down.

# NUGGET 05: GODLY LIVING

What is the will of God for my life? Let us explore some scriptures that state the will of God for our lives.

A person may not remember what you said but they will always remember how you made them feel. Your actions speak louder than your words. Are you living according to your profession? Do you practice what you preach? Can you be labeled a hypocrite?

> 1 Peter 2:15 (KJV) "For so is the will of God, that with well doing ye may put to silence the ignorance of foolish men. As free, and not using your liberty for a cloak of maliciousness, but as servants of God. Honour all men. Love the brotherhood. Fear God. Honour the king."

> I Peter 2:15-17 (NLT) "It is God's will that your honorable lives should silence those ignorant people who make foolish accusations against you. For you are free, yet you are God's slaves, so don't use your freedom as an excuse to do evil. Respect everyone and love the family of believers. Fear God and respect the king."

I Peter 2:15 (MSG) "It is God's will that by doing good, you might cure the ignorance of the fools who think you're a danger to society. Exercise your freedom by serving God, not by breaking the rules. Treat everyone you meet with dignity. Love your spiritual family. Revere God. Respect the government."

Hebrews 11:25 (KJV) "Choosing rather to suffer affliction with the people of God, than to enjoy the pleasures of sin for a season".

Hebrews 11:25 (NLT) "He chose to share the oppression of God's people instead of enjoying the fleeting pleasures of sin".

Hebrews 11:25 (MSG) "He chose a hard life with God's people rather than an opportunistic soft life of sin with the oppressors".

Here is the will of God for your life, simply put, let your well doing; that is your positive actions, silence the ignorance of foolish men. Foolish men are people who are lying and talking badly about you. You should live your life in such a way that if a person is lying on you, they would be hard pressed to find someone to believe them or even listen to them. You should live your life in such a way that you do not have the interest, the desire nor the need to prove them wrong because in your heart you know that

    1. they are lying,

2. you treat others right,
3. you are loving towards others despite how they treat you, and
4. you are living a life pleasing to the Lord.

As part of Godly living, we are not to retaliate against those who are lying on us. Nor are we to retaliate against those who are doing all kinds of things against us to make our lives miserable. Some may persecute us and stand against us for no apparent reason. However, we must stay focused on doing good, doing what is right in God's eyes and allow Him to fight that battle. Allow Him to repay them. Allow Him to seek the revenge.

> Deuteronomy 32:35 (KJV) "To me belongeth vengeance and recompence; their foot shall slide in due time; for the day of their calamity is at hand, and the things that shall come upon them make haste."

> Deuteronomy 32:35 (NLT) "I will take revenge; I will pay them back. In due time their feet will slip. Their day of disaster will arrive, and their destiny will overtake them."

> Deuteronomy 32:35 (NLV) "It is Mine to punish when their foot makes a false step. The day of their trouble is near. Their fall is coming fast upon them."

> Romans 12:19 (KJV) "Dearly beloved, avenge not yourselves, but rather give place unto wrath: for

it is written, Vengeance is mine; I will repay, saith the Lord."

Romans 12:19 (NIV) "Do not take revenge, my dear friends, but leave room for God's wrath, for it is written: "It is mine to avenge; I will repay,"[a] says the Lord."

Romans 12:19 (NLV) " Christian brothers, never pay back someone for the bad he has done to you. Let the anger of God take care of the other person. The Holy Writings say, "I will pay back to them what they should get, says the Lord."

Exodus 14:14 (KJV) "The Lord shall fight for you, and ye shall your peace."

Exodus 14:14 (NLT) "The Lord himself will fight for you. Just stay calm."

Exodus 14:14 (NLV) "The Lord will fight for you. All you have to do is keep still."

Deuteronomy 3:22 (KJV) "Ye shall not fear them: for the Lord your God he shall fight for you."

Deuteronomy 3:22 (NLT) "Do not be afraid of the nations there, for the Lord your God will fight for you."

Deuteronomy 3:22 (NLV) "Do not be afraid of them. For the Lord your God is the One fighting for you."

**Prayer of Release**

Heavenly Father help me to let go. Lord help me to give the battles of life and conflicts of this world to You. Help me Holy Spirit to open up my mind, heart and hands and give it freely to you. Lord, I pray that each day You go before me and fight each foe that is lying in wait for me. Thank you, God, for Your protection. Thank You, Lord, for each and every battle that You've fought on my behalf. Forgive me Lord for taking matters into my own hands. Forgive me for not trusting You Lord to handle it and handle them. I thank You Lord for Your grace and mercy. I thank You Lord that You neither slumber nor sleep therefore, even when I'm sleep You are protecting me. Thank You for covering me. I pray this prayer in the name of Jesus Christ. Amen.

**Life Application: "How can I cultivate a peace-maker attitude?"**

**Action Step:**

1. For 1 week, each night, pray for each person that is coming against you unjustly.

# NUGGET 06: SUFFERING FOR DOING GOOD

What is the will of God for my life? Let us explore some scriptures that state the will of God for our lives.

> I Peter 3:16-17 (KJV) "Having a good conscience; that, whereas they speak evil of you, as of evildoers, they may be ashamed that falsely accuse your good conversation in Christ. For it is better, if the will of God be so, that ye suffer for well doing, than for evil doing."

> I Peter 3:16-17 (NLT) "But do this in a gentle and respectful way. Keep your conscience clear. Then if people speak against you, they will be ashamed when they see what a good life you live because you belong to Christ. Remember, it is better to suffer for doing good, if that is what God's want, than to suffer for doing wrong!"

> I Peter 3: 13-17 (MSG) "If with heart and soul you're doing good, do you think you can be stopped? Even if you suffer for it, you're still better off. Don't give the opposition a second thought. Through thick

and thin, keep your hearts at attention, in adoration before Christ, your Master. Be ready to speak up and tell anyone who asks you why you're living the way you are, and always with the utmost courtesy. Keep a clear conscience before God so that when people throw mud at you, none of it will stick. They'll end up realizing that they're the ones who need a bath. It's better to suffer for doing good, if that's what God wants, then to be punished for doing bad."

Here is the will of God, simply put, accept that you may suffer even though you are doing what is right, in the sight of God. This might initially seem to be a shocker or even a point of discouragement, but trust that you are in a better position to suffer for well doing as opposed to suffering, rightfully so, for wrongdoing. Many Christians are asking, "Why God?" "Why am I suffering?" They are struggling to find fault or find an error in their living – confused and bewildered – they search, cry, and pray – for an answer – many times it does not come. This is a hard truth to swallow. You do not have to be disobedient or in sin to suffer. It is God's will, at times in our lives, that we suffer while doing good.

This is an example of the apostles suffering for doing what was right and rejoicing while going through the trial. They were honored to suffer for our Lord. They were not confused, because they knew their conduct was good and right in the sight of God.

Acts 5:40-41 (KJV) "And to him they agreed: and when they had called the apostles, and beaten them, they commanded that they should not speak in the name of Jesus and let them go. And they departed from the presence of the council, rejoicing that they were counted worthy to suffer shame for his name."

Acts 5:40-41 (NLT) "The others accepted his advice. They called in the apostles and had them flogged. Then they ordered them never again to speak in the name of Jesus, and they let them go. The apostles left the high council rejoicing that God had counted them worthy to suffer disgrace for the name of Jesus."

Acts 5:40-41 (MSG) "That convinced them. They called the apostles back in. After giving them a thorough whipping, they warned them not to speak in Jesus' name and sent them off. The apostle went out of the High Council overjoyed because they had been given the honor of being dishonored on account of the Name."

This is an example of the Lord telling Ananias that Saul, His chosen vessel, would suffer for being obedient to His will and His way.

Acts 9:15-16 (KJV) "But the Lord said unto him, go thy way: for he is a chosen vessel unto me, to bear my name before the Gentiles, and kings, and the children of Israel: For I will shew him how great things he must suffer for my name's sake."

Acts 9:15-16 (NLT) "But the Lord said "Go, for Saul is my chosen instrument to take my message to the Gentiles and to kings, as well as to the people of Israel. And I will show him how much he must suffer for my name's sake."

Acts 9:15-16 (MSG) "But the Master said "Don't argue. Go! I have picked him as my personal representative to non-Jews and kings and Jews. And now I'm about to show him what he's in for – the hard suffering that goes with this job."

This is an example of how Paul accepted suffering as part of his calling.

2 Timothy 1:11-12 (KJV) "Whereunto I am appointed a preacher, and an apostle, and a teacher of the Gentiles. For the which cause I also suffer these things: nevertheless, I am not ashamed: for I know whom I have believed and am persuaded that he is able to keep that which I have committed unto him against that day."

2 Timothy 1:11-12 (NLT) "And God chose me to be a preacher, an apostle, and a teacher of this Good News. That is why I am suffering here in prison. But I am not ashamed of it, for I know the one in whom

I trust, and I am sure that he is able to guard what I have entrusted to him until the day of his return."

2 Timothy 1:11-12 (MSG) "This is the Message I've been set apart to proclaim as preacher, emissary, and teacher. It's also the cause of all this trouble I'm in. But I have no regrets. I couldn't be surer of my ground – the One I've trusted in can take care of what he's trusted me to do right to the end."

Believers should also accept that we too will suffer for Christ.

Philippians 1:29 (KJV) "For unto you is given in the behalf of Christ, not only to believe on him, but also to suffer for his sake;"

Philippians 1:29 (NLT) "For you have been given not only the privilege of trusting in Christ but also the privilege of suffering for him".

Philippians 1:29 (MSG) "There's far more to this life than trusting in Christ. There's also suffering for him. And the suffering is as much as a gift as the trusting."

According to these verses, we are to have good conversations in Christ, that is, Godly conversations. By our conduct, we, Christians show that accusations against us are unfounded. Our conscience should be clear from any guilt.

If the will of God brings about some suffering upon us, then we will know this is His will and not be confused, because

1. We have been obedient in having Godly conversation,
2. Our conscience is clear that we have done no evil to the one speaking falsely against us and slandering our name,
3. People falsely accusing us does not bother us, and
4. Go back to #1.

Let's remember that Christ, being our ultimate example, suffered terribly for doing only what was right – the will of God. Christ was obedient in His lifestyle and in His speech all the way to the cross. On that journey, many hurled false accusations at Him.

God knew we would have to endure suffering during our lifetime. We are to put on the full armor of God each and every morning. Don't leave home without it.

> Ephesians 6:10-17 (KJV) "Finally, my brethren, be strong in the Lord, and in the power of his might. Put on the whole armour of God, that ye may be able to stand against the wiles of the devil. For we wrestle not against flesh and blood, but against principalities, against powers, against the rulers of the darkness of this world, against spiritual wickedness in high places. Wherefore take unto you the whole armour of God, that ye may be able to withstand

in the evil day, and having done all, to stand. Stand therefore, having your loins girt about with truth, and having on the breastplate of righteousness; And your feet shod with the preparation of the gospel of peace; Above all, taking the shield of faith, wherewith ye shall be able to quench all the fiery darts of the wicked. And take the helmet of salvation, and the sword of the Spirit, which is the word of God"

Ephesians 6:10-17 (NLT) "A final word: Be strong in the Lord and in his mighty power. Put on all of God's armor so that you will be able to stand firm against all strategies of the devil. For we[d] are not fighting against flesh-and-blood enemies, but against evil rulers and authorities of the unseen world, against mighty powers in this dark world, and against evil spirits in the heavenly places. Therefore, put on every piece of God's armor so you will be able to resist the enemy in the time of evil. Then after the battle you will still be standing firm. Stand your ground, putting on the belt of truth and the body armor of God's righteousness. For shoes, put on the peace that comes from the Good News so that you will be fully prepared. In addition to all of these, hold up the shield of faith to stop the fiery arrows of the devil. Put on salvation as your helmet, and take the sword of the Spirit, which is the word of God."

Ephesians 6:10-17 (NLV) "This is the last thing I want to say: Be strong with the Lord's strength. Put on the things God gives you to fight with. Then you will not fall into the traps of the devil. Our fight is not with people. It is against the leaders and the powers and the spirits of darkness in this world. It is against the demon world that works in the heavens. Because of this, put on all the things God gives you to fight with. Then you will be able to stand in that sinful day. When it is all over, you will still be standing. So stand up and do not be moved. Wear a belt of truth around your body. Wear a piece of iron over your chest which is being right with God. Wear shoes on your feet which are the Good News of peace. Most important of all, you need a covering of faith in front of you. This is to put out the fire-arrows of the devil. The covering for your head is that you have been saved from the punishment of sin. Take the sword of the Spirit which is the Word of God."

## Prayer of Strength

Heavenly Father strengthen my spirit and toughen my emotions such that I can have inner peace, joy and happiness in the midst of betrayal, lies and deception. Lord, I know that I can walk in victory with Your strength. Heavenly Father, I know Satan is the father of lies and no truth is within him, the defeated foe. I pray that each day, the Holy Spirit, helps me to be fully dressed for the battle of life. In Jesus Christ name, I pray this prayer. Amen.

**Life Application: "How can I cultivate a spirit of victory in the midst of the storm?"**

**Action Steps:**

1. Write down the victory that happened despite the struggle – the testimony.
2. For 1 week, each day, share your testimony with someone, of how, in the midst of suffering – God still got the Glory – God showed up and showed out - in a mighty, undeniable way.

# EPILOGUE

It is my hope and prayer that each of you will reach out to the Lord asking the Holy Spirit to empower you to exercise self-control, to display integrity and to have a cheerful servant's heart. All of these characteristics are needed in order to fulfill His will for your life. I have been taught, if you pray to the Lord to help you to be obedient or to be more obedient to His word, you are guaranteed that that specific prayer will be answered.

I will be the first to admit, from my personal experience, that change is not easy. Implementing these nuggets consistently into our daily lives will not be easy, however, God's word never said that walking consistently in His will would be easy. Jesus journey up Golgotha's hill was surely not easy. Just because change might be a challenge, does not mean change is not attainable.

> Romans 6:12-14 (KJV) "Let not sin therefore reign in your mortal body, that ye should obey it in the lusts thereof. Neither yield ye your members as instruments of unrighteousness unto sin: but yield yourselves unto God, as those that are alive from the dead, and your members as instruments

of righteousness unto God. For sin shall not have dominion over you: for ye are not under the law, but under grace.

Romans 6:12-14 (NLT) "Do not let sin control the way you live; do not give in to sinful desires. Do not let any part of your body become an instrument of evil to serve sin. Instead, give yourselves completely to God, for you were dead, but now you have new life. So use your whole body as an instrument to do what is right for the glory of God. Sin is no longer your master, for you no longer live under the requirements of the law. Instead, you live under the freedom of God's grace."

Romans 6:12-14 (MSG) "That means you must not give sin a vote in the way you conduct your lives. Don't give it the time of day. Don't even run little errands that are connected with that old way of life. Throw yourselves wholeheartedly and full time – remember, you've been raised from the dead! – into God's way of doing things. Sin can't tell you how to live. After all, you're not living under that old tyranny any longer. You're living in the freedom of God."

I have enjoyed sharing these breakfast nuggets with you. Let me end our meal with an encouraging scripture. If you desire to change, our Lord can change you. He wants us to be obedient, and He gives us His Holy Spirit to help us to walk and live in obedience. He is the Potter, and we are the clay. He can reshape and remold us as needed. Allow Him to make over those weak areas of your life today. Just ask Him! Nothing is too hard for God nor is anything impossible for Him. You can become a new creature in Christ. You can walk and live in His will.

Luke 1:37 (KJV) "For with God nothing shall be impossible".

Luke 1:37 (NLT) "For the word of God will never fail".

Luke 1:37 (MSG) "Nothing, you see, is impossible with God. "

# MY CLOSING PRAYER

It is my prayer and hope that each and every person who reads this book, will be so moved, enlightened, helped, and inspired that they will be compelled to share this book with others. Don't keep the will of God a secret. Bless someone. Spread it throughout all the communities, cities, states, world, and countries.

I pray that it is your desire to have your thoughts, your speech, your actions and your life aligned with the will of God.

There are many benefits to doing the will of God.

We should find joy in doing the will of God. Living a Christian life, should not be boring, dreaded, burdensome nor sorrowful, but an exciting, cheerful and joyful life. God's way is always the right way. What is in our heart – comes out of our mouth and shows in our behavior. (Luke 6:45, Proverbs 4:23, Matthew 15:18)

Isn't it awesome to have our Lord's instructions written on our hearts? Then there will be an outpouring of love, patience, kindness, gentleness, long suffering…the list goes on (Galatians 5:22-23)

Psalms 40:8(KJV) "I delight to do thy will, O my God: yea, thy law is within my heart."

Psalms 40:8 (NLT) "I take joy in doing your will, my God for your instructions are written on my heart."

Psalms 40:8(MSG) "That's when God's Word entered my life, became part of my very being."

Our Lord wants us to do His will, and He will teach us what His will is. We don't have to struggle with it. Ask the Lord to give you the desire to do His will and then teach you to carry it out. This is a request and prayer that is sure to be answered. God will never ask us to do something that He does not equip us to do. It is okay to be F.A.T. for the Lord – Faithful, Available, Teachable.

Psalms 143:10(KJV) "Teach me to do thy will; for thou are my God: thy spirit is good; lead me into the land of uprightness."

Psalms 143:10 (NLT) "Teach me to do your will, for you are my God. May your gracious Spirit lead me forward on a firm footing."

Psalms 143:10(MSG) "Teach me how to live to please you, because you're my God. Lead me by your blessed Spirit into cleared and level pastureland."

I Kings 8:58(KJV) "That he may incline our hearts unto him, to walk in all his ways, and to keep his commandments, and his statues, and his judgments, which he commanded our fathers."

I Kings 8:58 (NLT) "May he give us the desire to do his will in everything and to obey all the commands, decrees, and regulations that he gave our ancestors"

I Kings 8:58(MSG) "May he keep us centered and devoted to him, following the life path he has cleared, watching the signposts, walking at the pace and rhythms he laid down for our ancestors."

Hebrews 13:21(KJV) "Make you perfect in every good work to do his will, working in you that which is well pleasing in his sight, through Jesus Christ; to whom be glory forever and ever. Amen"

Hebrews 13:21(NLT) "May he equip you with all you need for doing his will. May he produce in you, through the power of Jesus Christ, every good thing that is pleasing to him. All glory to him forever and ever! Amen."

Hebrews 13:21(MSG) "Now put you together, provide you with everything you need to please him. Make us into what gives him most pleasure, by means of the sacrifice of Jesus, the Messiah. All glory to Jesus forever and always! Oh, yes, yes, yes."

Decisions, decisions, decisions. Each day, we have to make decisions. Allow our Lord to direct your path. When you walk in His will, your pathway will be clear. The steps of a good man are ordered by the Lord. (Psalms

37:23) Seek His will. Listen for His voice. Acknowledge Him in all of your situations.

Proverbs 3:6(KJV) "In all thy ways acknowledge him, and he shall direct thy paths."

Proverbs 3:6 (NLT) "Seek his will in all you do, and he will show you which path to take.

Proverbs 3:6(MSG) "Listen for God's voice in everything you do, everywhere you go; he's the one who will keep you on track."

We all pray, and we all want answers to our prayers! No one wants their words to just bounce around off the walls of their room! God hears the prayers of His Children who are doing in His will. What a huge benefit – a great perk – an awesome reward.

John 9:31(KJV) "Now we know that God heareth not sinners: but if any man be a worshipper of God, an doeth his will, him he heareth."

John 9:31(NLT) "We know that God doesn't listen to sinners, but he is ready to hear those who worship him and do his will".

John 9:31(MSG) "It's well known that God isn't at the beck and call of sinners but listens carefully to anyone who lives in reverences and does his will."

You will be a blessing to others when doing the will of God. You will be able to comfort those that are weary.

Our Lord will bless you with wisdom and understanding and you will in turn be a blessing to others. This is a win – win situation. Each day, the Lord allows us to wake up is an opportunity to be a blessing to someone else. Let's not take this opportunity lightly.

Isaiah 50:4(KJV) "The Lord God hath given me the tongue of the learned, that I should know how to speak a word in season to him that is weary: he wakeneth morning by morning, he wakeneth mine ear to hear as the learned."

Isaiah 50:4(NLT) "The Sovereign Lord has given me his words of wisdom, so that I know how to comfort the weary. Morning by morning he wakens me and opens my understanding to his will."

Isaiah 50:4(MSG) "The Master, God, has given me a well-taught tongue, so I know how to encourage tired people. He wakes me up in the morning, Wakes me up, opens my ears to listen as one ready to take orders."

Ask others to agree with you in prayer that you be filled with the knowledge of the will of God. Declare that you are ready to die to yourself and be born again into living a life according to the will of God. The prayers of the righteous availeth much. (James 5:16)

Colossians 1:9(KJV) "For this cause we also, since the day we heard it, do not cease to pray for you, and to desire that ye might be filled with the knowledge of his will in all wisdom and spiritual understanding."

Colossians 1:9(NLT) "So we have not stopped praying for you since we first heard about you. We ask God to give you complete knowledge of his will and to give you spiritual wisdom and understanding."

Colossians 1:9(MSG) "Be assured that from the first day we heard of you, we haven't stopped praying for you, asking God to give you wise minds and spirits attuned to his will, and so acquire a thorough understanding of the ways in which God works."

# Appendix A – The Plan of Salvation

God calls believers at least twice. First, He calls people out of the darkness of sin into the light of salvation through the redemptive work of His Son on the cross. Secondly, He calls the believer into service through the indwelling presence and power of His Holy Spirit.

The faith that we have is not for us to keep. We are to share it. Share your faith today with those you encounter. This too is the will of God for our lives.

God wants everyone to be saved:

2 Peter 3:9 (KJV) "The Lord is not slack concerning his promise, as some men count slackness; but is longsuffering to us-ward, not willing that any should perish, but that all should come to repentance."

2 Peter 3:9 (NLT) "The Lord isn't really being slow about his promise, as some people think. No, he is being patient for your sake. He does not want anyone to be destroyed but wants everyone to repent."

2 Peter 3:9 (MSG) "God isn't late with his promise as some measure lateness. He is restraining himself on account of you, holding back the End because he doesn't want anyone lost. He's giving everyone space and time to change."

We have been commanded to spread the gospel to the entire world.

Matthew 28:19 (KJV) "Go ye therefore, and teach all nations, baptizing them in the name of the Father, and of the Son, and of the Holy Spirit."

Matthew 28:19 (NLT) "Therefore, go and make disciples of all the nations, baptizing them in the name of the Father and the son and the Holy Spirit."

Matthew 28:19 (MSG) "... Go out and train everyone you meet, far and near, in this way of life, marking them by baptism in the threefold name: Father, Son, and Holy Spirit."

Once we share how Christ died on the cross for the world – He will do the drawing. We cannot save anyone. We are only called to share the good news of the Gospel.

John 12:32 (KJV) "And I, if I be lifted up from the earth, will draw all men unto me".

John 12:32 (NLT) "And when I am lifted up from the earth, I will draw everyone to myself"

John 12:32 (MSG) "… And I as I am lifted up from the earth, will attract everyone to me and gather them around me."

Following are various ways to share the plan of salvation to the world.

# F.A.I.T.H.

We need God's **Forgiveness**

God is **Available** but not **Automatic**

It is **Impossible** to allow sin into Heaven, so we must

**Turn** to God

In order to have **Heaven**

# B.A.T.

**Believe** (Romans 3:23)

> That you have sinned against God and that Jesus can save you

**Ask** (I John 1:9)

> Ask Jesus to forgive you and make your heart clean

**Tell** (Romans 10:9)

> Tell Jesus that you want Him to be Lord of your life

# A.B.C.

**Admit** (Romans 3:23, Isaiah 53:6)

1. That you have made mistakes
2. That you are a sinner in need of forgiveness

**Believe** (John 3:16, Romans 5:8)

1. That Jesus is God's only Son, and He chose to die on a cross for you
2. That Jesus Christ died for your sins
3. That you have sinned against God and that Jesus can save you

**Commit** (Romans 10:9, Acts 3:19)

1. Yourself to a life of following Jesus and serving others

# G.O.S.P.E.L.

**G** - **G**od created us to be with Him

**O** - **O**ur sins separates us from God

**S** - **S**ins cannot be removed by good deeds

**P** - **P**aying the price for sin, Jesus died and rose again

**E** - **E**veryone who trusts in Him alone has eternal life

**L** - **L**ife with Jesus starts now and lasts forever

# T.R.U.S.T.

**T** - Turn from your wicked ways

**R** - Repent of your Sins

**U** - Understand that you cannot enter heaven alone

**S** - Seek the saving power of Jesus

**T** - Take God at his Word

## The Gospel Story Shared By Colors

**Black** represents separation caused by sin

"For all have sinned and come short of the glory of God" Romans 3:23

**Red** represents the blood of Jesus shed on the cross

"While we were yet sinners, Christ died for us" Romans 5:8

**Blue** represents the baptism

"We were buried with Him thru baptism" Romans 5:4, Acts 2:41

**White** represents being cleaned and forgiven

"Wash me and I shall be whiter than snow" Psalm 51:7, Isaiah 1:18

**Green** represents growth in God's love

"Grow in grace and in the knowledge of our Lord and Savior Jesus Christ", 2 Peter 3:18

**Yellow** represents the crown of eternal life

"Be faithful until death and I will give you a crown of life" Revelations 2:10, John 3:16

# APPENDIX B - SPIRITUALLY RELATED ACRONYMS

**Note: Before using of any of these acronyms, it is your legal obligation to research them, in order to determine if they have been trademarked.**

A

A.D.D. – Anointed Devoted Disciples

A.D.D. – Anointed Dedicated Disciples

A.B.C. – Always Being Cheerful

B

B.I.G. – Beautiful In God

B.I.G. – Believer in God

B.I.G. – Balm in Gilead

B.I.G. – Bold in God

B.A.S.I.C. – Becoming a Soldier in Christ

C

C.O.U.P.L.E. - Christ Offering Ultimate Peace Love and Encouragement

C.I.A. – Christ is Alive

D

D.I.V.A. – Divinely Inspired Virtuously Anointed

D.O.G. – Disciple of God

D.O.G. – Depending on God

D.O.G. – Delay of Gratification

D.A.D. – Dedicated and Devoted

D.A.D. – Decide Announce Defend

D.A.D. – Defenders against Demons

D.A.D. – Defenders against the Devil

D.A.D. – Disciples Anointed Devoted

D.O.P.E. – Depending on Prayer Everyday

E

E.G.O. – Exiting God Out

F

F.R.O.G. – Firmly Relying on God

F.R.O.G. – Fully Relying on God

F.R.O.G. – Forever Relying on God

F.R.O.G. – Faithfully Relying on God

F.E.A.R. – False Expectation Appearing Real

F.B.I. – Firm Believer in Christ

F.B.I. – Firm Believer in Jesus

F.A.T. – Faithful Available Teachable

F.A.T. – Faithful and True

F. A. I .T. H. – Forwarding All Issue To Him

G

G.P.S. – God's Plan of Salvation

H

H.A.L.T. – Hungry Angry Lonely Tired

H.A.N.D. – Have A Nice Day

H.E.L.P. – His Ever Loving Presence

H.E.L.P. – His Everlasting Loving Protection

H.E.L.P. – His Everlasting Loving Provision

H.E.L.P. - Humbly Expecting Life's Promises

I

J

J.O.Y. – Jesus Others Yourself

K

L

L.E.T.G.O. – Leave Everything to God Only

L.O.V.E. – Loving Others Victoriously Everyday

M

M.O.M. – Men on a Mission

M.O.M. – Mothers on a Mission

M.O.M. – Mothers Ordained for Ministry

M.O.M. – Men Ordained for Ministry

M.O.M. – Made of Miracles

M.O.M. – Maker of Me

M.O.P. – Men of Praise

M.O.P. – Men of Purpose

N

N.O.W. – No Other Way

O

P

P.I.T. – Pulling It Together

P.U.S.H. – Pray Until Something Happens

P.U.S.H. – Praise Until Something Happens

P.R.A.Y. – Praise Repent Ask and Yield

Q

R

R.E.N.E.W. – Respecting Educating Nurturing Empowering Women

R.E.A.D – Renewing Empowering Anointing Delivering

R.E.A.D. – Revealing Empowering Action Determined

R.E.A.D. – Read Enjoy and Discover

S

S.T.E.M. – Saved Tested Edified Manifested

S.O.S. – Save Our Souls

S.T.O.P. – Stop Think Observe Pray

S.W.A.G. – Someone Who Adores God

S.W.A.G. – Sisters Who Adores God

T

U

V

W

W.O.G. – Woman of God

W.W.W. – When Women Worship

W.O.W. – Woman of Worth

X

Y

Y.C.A. – Young Christians in Action

Z